by Glenn McCoy
Foreword by Lynn Johnston

**Andrews McMeel
Publishing**

Kansas City

ISBN: 0-8362-5185-7

Library of Congress Catalog Card Number: 97-74518

Foreword

Glenn McCoy not only writes funny (some of his E's look like R's), he draws the kind of boneless, goofy, impossible characters that stick in your mind like bugs to flypaper.

His cartoon assembly: Eno, his dog Fang, their landlady Gina, and her poodle-pal Mitzi, coexist in *The Duplex*—an impossible dwelling in an impossible world.

Is their creator crazy? It's possible! That's why this very funny and hilariously drawn comic strip is such a good read. Here is a glimpse into the mind of a man who can make other cartoonists laugh and who can evoke the most cherished of compliments: Why didn't *I* think of that?!!

Glenn McCoy's syndicated strip is a new and very welcome addition to the newspaper comics page—keeping it still, the first page most people turn to for comfort and comedy.

Now, turn this page, give way to your imagination, and enter *The Duplex*. Don't be surprised if it feels like home!

—Lynn Johnston, creator of *For Better or For Worse*

For Mom and Dad.
The three people who
taught me how to count.

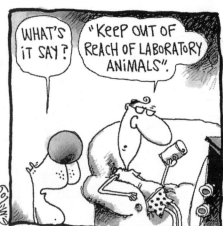

SEE? IT'S A LITTLE DINING ROOM SET! I MADE IT WITH TOOTHPICKS AND GLUE. THE CHINA CABINET STILL NEEDS A COUPLE MORE COATS OF STAIN.

UH, FANG...

THE SOFA WAS A LITTLE TRICKIER. TOOK ME A WHOLE WEEK TO MAKE. IT ACTUALLY FOLDS OUT INTO A LITTLE BED! NOW HERE'S SOME MATERIAL I WAS CONSIDERING FOR—

FANG! FANG!

I THINK I SHOULD EXPLAIN SOMETHING ABOUT THAT ROACH MOTEL I PUT IN THE KITCHEN.

ENO HAS A CRUSH ON THAT BLOND GIRL WHO MOVED IN DOWN THE STREET.

IS SHE PRETTY?

DO THE NUMBERS 36-24-36 MEAN ANYTHING TO YOU?

THOSE ARE HER MEASUREMENTS, HUH?

NO, THAT'S ENO'S WAIST SIZE BEFORE, DURING, AND AFTER SHE WALKS BY.

WHAT'LL IT BE?

TAKE A LITTLE OFF THE TOP.

WHAT'LL IT BE?

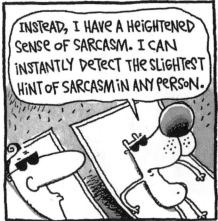

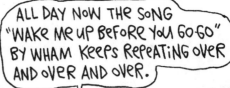

100 WAYS TO TELL iF YOU'RE A LOSER...

#1. You refuse to believe that the Partridge Family used to lip-sync their songs.

It's a fact!

Fighting words!

#2. You coordinate your wardrobe around the "kick me" signs taped to your back.

Ooh! That one will go great with your blue pull-over!

Ya think so?

100 WAYS TO TELL iF YOU'RE A LOSER...

#3. You bought a copy of Richard Simmons' "Sweating to the '70s" workout tape just for the rockin' tunes.

♫ Dancing Queen... ♫

#4. Your idea of making a radical fashion statement is mixing reptile and marsupial Garanimals.

AUGH!

100 WAYS TO TELL iF YOU'RE A LOSER...

#5. If you've ever been bodily removed from a karaoke stage.

♫ ...That's the night that the lights went out in Georgia... ♫

BOUNCER

#6. You get upset with the obvious media bias of the "Hard Copy" news coverage.

It's been two weeks and not one story about Ricki Lake's latest tummy tuck!!

It's a coverup!

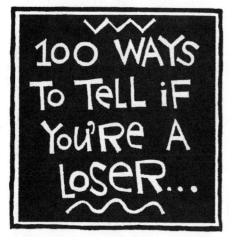

100 WAYS TO TELL IF YOU'RE A LOSER...

#7. IF YOU'VE EVER MISSED COMPLETELY TRYING TO GIVE A HIGH FIVE.

WOW! WHAT AN INCREDIBLE CATCH!!

#8. YOU CAN RECITE FROM THE TV GUIDE VERBATIM.

ANYTHING GOOD ON TV TONIGHT?

YEAH. AT 6 O'CLOCK ON "SAVED BY THE BELL", SCREETCH SNAPS AFTER BEING CAUGHT CHEATING ON AN EXAM AND HOLDS HIS CLASS HOSTAGE WITH A LAWN JART. (R) (CC)

100 WAYS TO TELL IF YOU'RE A LOSER...

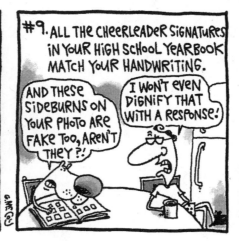

#9. ALL THE CHEERLEADER SIGNATURES IN YOUR HIGH SCHOOL YEARBOOK MATCH YOUR HANDWRITING.

AND THESE SIDEBURNS ON YOUR PHOTO ARE FAKE TOO, AREN'T THEY?!

I WON'T EVEN DIGNIFY THAT WITH A RESPONSE!

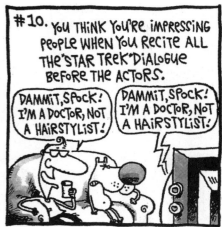

#10. YOU THINK YOU'RE IMPRESSING PEOPLE WHEN YOU RECITE ALL THE "STAR TREK" DIALOGUE BEFORE THE ACTORS.

DAMMIT, SPOCK! I'M A DOCTOR, NOT A HAIRSTYLIST!

DAMMIT, SPOCK! I'M A DOCTOR, NOT A HAIRSTYLIST!

100 WAYS TO TELL IF YOU'RE A LOSER...

#11. YOU STEAL CABLE TO GET THE WEATHER CHANNEL.

THAT'S THE SECOND HIGH PRESSURE ZONE IN THREE DAYS.

MUST BE SWEEPS WEEK.

#12. WAL-MART GREETERS AVOID YOU.

...AND I'LL TELL YOU ANOTHER REASON WHY "MATLOCK'S" GOING DOWNHILL.

SHUT UP!! LEAVE ME ALONE!

21

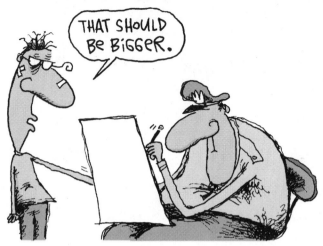

22

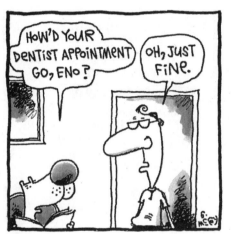

100 WAYS TO TELL IF YOU'RE A LOSER...

#13. BEFORE BUYING A NEW PAIR OF SHOES, YOU FIRST HAVE TO SEE HOW THEY LOOK WITH TOILET PAPER STUCK TO THE BOTTOM.

HMM... COULD I SEE THIS SHOE WITH A 2-PLY?

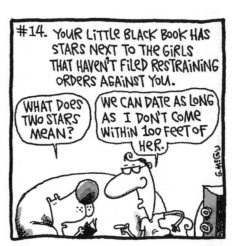

#14. YOUR LITTLE BLACK BOOK HAS STARS NEXT TO THE GIRLS THAT HAVEN'T FILED RESTRAINING ORDERS AGAINST YOU.

WHAT DOES TWO STARS MEAN?

WE CAN DATE AS LONG AS I DON'T COME WITHIN 100 FEET OF HER.

HOW'S YOUR TV COMMERCIAL ACTING CAREER GOING, ELVIN?

I GUESS IT WASN'T MEANT TO BE, GINA.

WHAT HAPPENED?

I WAS ON MY WAY TO SHOOT ONE OF THOSE BLINDFOLDED TASTE TESTS.

AND I DROVE MY CAR INTO A TELEPHONE POLE.

100 WAYS TO TELL IF YOU'RE A LOSER...

OOH! OW!! I GOT SOAP IN MY EYES! OUCH, IT BURNS!! QUICK, HAND ME A TOWEL!!!

HERE Y'GO.

AUGHHH!!

WAIT, DID YOU SAY 'TOWEL' OR 'DIRTY TUBE SOCKS'?

DID YOU EVER NOTICE HOW THE NICE GUYS NEVER GET THE GIRLS? WOMEN JUST DON'T GO FOR HONEST, GOOD-HEARTED GUYS.

IT'S REALLY UNFAIR!

I MEAN, THE WAY I SEE IT, WOMEN JUST DON'T REALIZE WHAT A BIG JERK I AM!

WHAT'S THIS, FANG?

IT'S A PAINTING I DID THIS AFTERNOON. I WAS WATCHING ONE OF THOSE HOW-TO-PAINT SHOWS ON TV.

THE INSTRUCTOR TAKES YOU STEP-BY-STEP THROUGH PAINTING A PICTURE. YOU JUST DO WHAT HE DOES. TODAY'S SHOW WAS ON "HOW TO PAINT SNOW-CAPPED MOUNTAINS."

WHAT'S WITH ALL THE BLOND GIRLS IN BIKINIS?

ENO SWITCHED ON "BAYWATCH" HALFWAY INTO THE SHOW.

COUGH. SNORT. SPLURT. SNIFFLE. SNORT. SNORT.

WOW! IS THERE ANYTHING MORE EMBARRASSING THAN GAGGING ON A BIG NOSE FULL OF WATER AFTER A DIVE?

WHAT'RE YOU DRINKING?

UH, PEPSI-FREE PEPSI.

PEPSI-FREE PEPSI?

YEAH. IT'S JUST SUGAR AND CAFFEINE.

CALL 911! CALL 911!

LOOKS LIKE THE CABLE WENT OUT DURING "BAYWATCH" AGAIN.

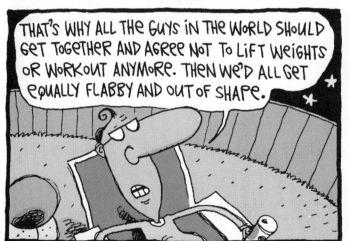

37

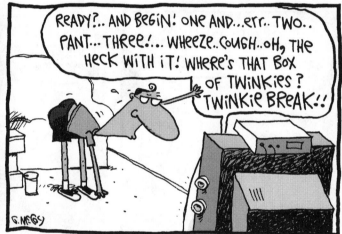

YOU KNOW, FANG, I LOVE MY MOM. I MEAN, SHE'S THE GREATEST MOM IN THE WORLD...

BUT SOMETIMES I FEEL SHE WON'T LET ME GROW UP! SHE STILL TREATS ME LIKE I'M A LITTLE KID.

SHE'S ALWAYS CHECKING UP ON ME AND REMINDING ME TO DO THINGS LIKE I'M AN IDIOT OR SOMETHING.

I'M AN ADULT NOW AND I DESERVE TO BE TREATED LIKE ONE. Y'KNOW, IT REALLY BUGS ME SOMETIMES.

WHY DON'T YOU TELL HER THIS?

DO YOU REALLY THINK I SHOULD?

DEFINITELY. GET OUT OF BED AND GIVE HER A CALL.

NO. I'LL JUST TELL HER OVER MY MR. BUNNY BABY MONITOR.

50

51

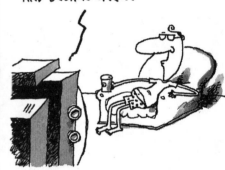

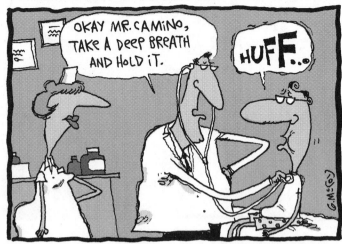

WHEN I WAS LITTLE, THERE WAS THIS EIGHT-YEAR-OLD WHO WOULD ALWAYS WAIT AT THE STREET CORNER AND TAKE MY QUARTER. I REMEMBER I COULDN'T WAIT TILL I GREW UP SO THINGS WOULD BE DIFFERENT.

BUT YOU KNOW, THEY REALLY AREN'T.

YOU MEAN THERE ARE ADULTS WHO CAN BE JUST AS BULLYING THROUGH AUTHORITY OR ECONOMIC POWER?

NO, I MEAN THERE'S STILL SOME EIGHT-YEAR-OLD DOWN THE STREET THAT KEEPS TAKING MY QUARTERS.

Y'KNOW, RACHEL, FOR A FIRST DATE I THINK THIS WENT PRETTY WELL. HOW 'BOUT A GOODNIGHT KISS?

WAIT! STEP BACK! I DROPPED ONE OF MY CONTACTS!!

CONTACTS? YOU'RE WEARING GLASSES!

OOOH! LEG CRAMP!!

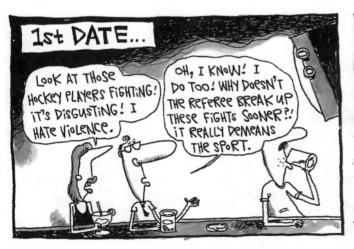

1st DATE...

LOOK AT THOSE HOCKEY PLAYERS FIGHTING! IT'S DISGUSTING! I HATE VIOLENCE.

OH, I KNOW! I DO TOO! WHY DOESN'T THE REFEREE BREAK UP THESE FIGHTS SOONER?! IT REALLY DEMEANS THE SPORT.

5th DATE

LOOK AT THOSE HOCK...

KILL HIM!! THE HEAD! GO FOR THE HEAD!

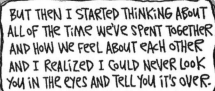

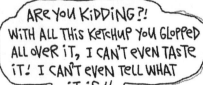

I DON'T KNOW, FANG. I WANT TO ASK THAT GIRL AT THE END OF THE BAR OUT FOR A DATE.

BUT EVERY TIME I TRY TO TALK TO HER SHE SLAPS ME ACROSS MY FACE. THE LAST TIME SHE BROKE MY NOSE IN SIX PLACES.

JUST REMEMBER ONE THING, ENO. BE POSITIVE.

WOW! YOU'RE RIGHT, FANG! THAT'S JUST THE TYPE OF ENCOURAGEMENT I NEEDED.

YES SIR! I CAN ALWAYS COUNT ON MY GOOD BUDDY FANG FOR SOME INSPIRING ADVICE. 'BE POSITIVE!' - THAT'S JUST WHAT I'LL DO!

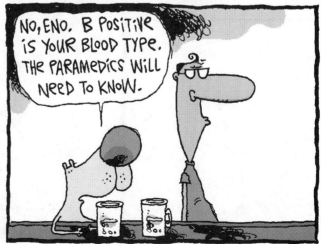

NO, ENO. B POSITIVE IS YOUR BLOOD TYPE. THE PARAMEDICS WILL NEED TO KNOW.

IT'S AMAZING HOW A PAIR OF SWIMMING TRUNKS I COULD BARELY FIT MY BUTT INTO BACK IN THE DRESSING ROOM...

CAN SUDDENLY HOLD ABOUT 2000 CUBIC FEET OF AIR ONCE YOU JUMP IN THE POOL!!

ELVIN, DID YOU ACTUALLY EAT THREE WHOLE BAGS OF OREOS AT ONE SITTING?

YEAH. FOOD HELPS ME KEEP MY MIND OFF OF SMOKING. IT'S SORT OF A SUBSTITUTE FOR CIGARETTES.

BUT YOU DON'T SMOKE! YOU'VE NEVER SMOKED!!

YEAH. IT'S SORT OF A PREVENTIVE MEASURE.

FANG, MY BEER IS GONE! WHERE'S MY BEER?!!

I PUT IT OUT IN OUR GARDEN.

YOU WHAT?!!

I PUT IT IN OUR VEGETABLE GARDEN. IT'S A WAY TO GET RID OF SLUGS.

Y'SEE, YOU SET OUT LITTLE BOWLS OF BEER. SLUGS ARE ATTRACTED TO BEER SO THEY CRAWL IN THE BOWLS AND DROWN.

UH, JUST HOW MANY LITTLE BOWLS OF BEER DID YOU SET OUT?

FOUR HUNDRED AND THIRTY.

I GUESS THAT EXPLAINS WHY ELVIN IS PASSED OUT IN OUR GREEN PEPPERS.

74

KNOCK
KNOCK

77

WHAT'CHA DOING, ENO?

WHAT'S IT LOOK LIKE?! I'M WATCHING ONE OF THOSE STEP-BY-STEP PAINTING SHOWS.

WHAT'S IT SUPPOSED TO BE?

IT'S NOT SUPPOSED TO BE ANYTHING! THIS EPISODE IS ON ABSTRACT ART. IT'S VERY HIGHBROW STUFF.

I DON'T GET IT.

OF COURSE YOU DON'T. I WOULDN'T EXPECT YOUR PUNY DOG BRAIN TO BE ABLE TO GRASP THE INTELLECTUAL NUANCES OF NON-REPRESENTATIONAL PAINTING.

JIGGLE JIGGLE

HEY, IT'S A BARN!

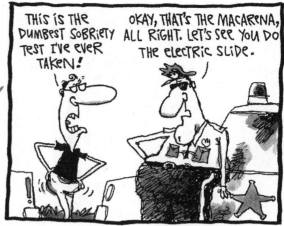

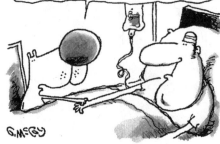

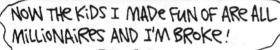

CLANK CLANK CLANK

89

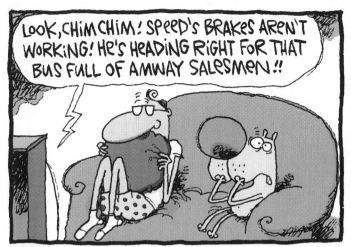

GREAT! YOU GET IN THE EXPRESS LINE TO SAVE TIME AND YOU GET STUCK BEHIND SOME IDIOT WHO CAN'T FIND HIS MONEY!!

NOW HE'S WRITING A CHECK! THIS'LL TAKE FOREVER! BOY, IT NEVER FAILS!

GREAT! MY BANANAS TURNED BLACK!!

HERE Y'GO, FANG. I STOPPED BY THE PET SUPPLY AISLE AT WAL-MART TODAY AND I BOUGHT YOU A CHEW TOY. IT SQUEAKS WHEN YOU BITE IT.

WHY?

HERE'S A 'DEAR ABBY' COLUMN I CUT OUT. SHE TELLS SOME BOZO NOT TO LEAVE HIS DIRTY SOCKS AND UNDERWEAR LYING AROUND HIS APARTMENT.

HERE'S AN 'ANN LANDERS' COLUMN WHERE SHE TELLS SOME JERK TO QUIT BEING SUCH A NEAT FREAK AND GET A LIFE.

TOUCHÉ.

I'D LIKE A CHEESY-BACON OMELETTE SANDWICH.

SORRY. WE STOPPED SERVING BREAKFAST THREE SECONDS AGO.

WAP

HEY, HANDS OFF THE HAIR NET!!

...AND WITH AUTOMATIC TRANSMISSION, LEATHER SEATS AND FACTORING IN THE MANUFACTURER'S REBATE, YOU CAN HAVE THIS LITTLE NUMBER FOR ONLY $16,499!

USED CARS

click click click

THAT COMES OUT TO 12 BILLION ALUMINUM BEER CANS.

CAN YOU HOLD IT FOR A COUPLE OF WEEKS?

THAT GUY AT THE END OF THE BAR IS GETTING PRETTY BELLIGERENT. I'M GOING TO GO TELL HIM TO SHUT HIS BIG MOUTH.

ARE YOU CRAZY?! THE GUY'S A GORILLA! HE'LL RIP YOUR EARS OFF!!

I'LL HAVE YOU KNOW I'M A MASTER OF HAND-TO-HAND COMBAT!

NO YOU'RE NOT!! REMEMBER? YOU'RE A MASTER AT HAND-TO-ARMPIT NOISES.

OH, YEAH.

WOW! LOOK AT BASSET'S YARD! HE'S SURE LETTING IT GO TO THE DOGS!

AHEM!

OOPS. SORRY. I GUESS PHRASES LIKE THAT ARE KIND OF INSULTING, HUH?

THAT'S OKAY. WE DOGS HAVE OUR SNIDE TERMS FOR PEOPLE, TOO, Y'KNOW.

REALLY? LIKE WHAT?

WE CALL'EM TWO-LEGGED HAIRLESS POOP SCOOPERS.

HMM... THIS IS INTERESTING. ACCORDING TO THIS ARTICLE, THE ARTIST FORMERLY KNOWN AS PRINCE IS CHANGING HIS NAME BACK.

YOU MEAN HE'S GOING BY 'PRINCE' AGAIN?

NO. NOW HE WANTS TO BE REFERRED TO AS 'THE ARTIST WHO UNTIL RECENTLY WAS KNOWN AS THE ARTIST FORMERLY KNOWN AS PRINCE.'

CATCHY.

TOMORROW IS MY FRIEND DEBBIE MUSICK'S BIRTHDAY.

OH YEAH. SHE TURNS THIRTY, RIGHT?

YEAH. AND I'M A LITTLE WORRIED. SOME WOMEN GET DEPRESSED WHEN THEY REACH SUCH A BIG MARK IN THEIR LIVES.

I KNOW WHAT YOU MEAN.

IT WAS THE SAME WAY FOR MY SISTER WHEN SHE SWITCHED FROM CYCLE ONE DOGFOOD TO CYCLE TWO.

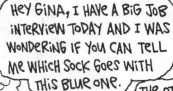

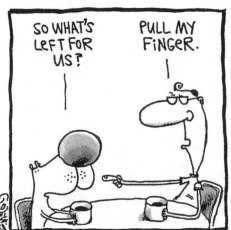

The Supreme Court dead-locked on whether it was constitutional for these strips to be censored. (Justice O'Connor wanted me caned.)